A WINNING SKILLS BOOK

You Can Be Assertive!

Joy Berry

Illustrated by Bartholomew

Copyright © Joy Berry, 2022
Originally Published 2013

All rights are reserved.

No part of this book can be duplicated or used without the prior written permission of the copyright owner, except for the use of brief quotations from the book.

For inquiries or permission requests contact the publisher.

Published by Joy Berry Enterprises
www.joyberryenterprises.com

Joy Berry Enterprises

To say no appropriately you need to know
- the power of "no,"
- when to say no,
- when not to say no,
- guidelines for saying no, and
- important sayings that relate to saying no.

THE POWER OF "NO"

"No" is one of the smallest words in the English language.

Even though the word "no" is small, it is very powerful.

THE POWER OF "NO"

The word "no" can stop a person from doing something.

The word "no" can stop a person from having something.

Most people do not like to be told that they cannot do something or have something. They do not want to be told no.

Because most people do not like to be told no, you might find that saying no is difficult.

Even though saying no might be difficult, there are times when it is necessary for you to do so.

When you are asked to do something that is wrong, you need to say no.

WHEN TO SAY NO

You need to say no when someone asks you to do something that you are not able to do.

When you are asked to do something that you do not want to do, you need to say no.

WHEN TO SAY NO

You need to say no when people offer to do something for you that you do not want them to do.

When people ask you to give them something that you do not want to give them, you need to say no.

WHEN TO SAY NO

You need to say now when someone offers you something that you do not want.

When you are asked whether you understand something that you do not understand, you need to say no.

WHEN TO SAY NO

You need to say no when someone asks whether you agree if you do not agree.

When you are asked whether you like something that you do not like, you need to say no.

You need to say no when you are asked whether you feel the way someone else thinks you should feel if you do not feel that way.

When you are asked to be with someone you don't want to be with, you need to say no.

WHEN NOT TO SAY NO

There are times when you should say no. There are also times when you should not say no.

Do not say no when you are asked to stop doing something that will hurt you or another person.

Do not say no when someone asks you to do something for your safety or the safety of others.

WHEN NOT TO SAY NO

Do not say no when you are asked to do something that you are supposed to do.

Do not say no when saying no is a lie.

GUIDELINES FOR SAYING NO

If and when you need to say no, you need to do it appropriately. You can accomplish this by following six guidelines.

Guideline One. Get the facts.

Find out exactly what the question is.

Find out what will happen if you say yes and if you say no.

Also find out exactly what you will be expected to do if you say yes and if you say no.

Guideline Two. Think about it.

Think about how your decision might affect you or others.

Ask yourself, "How will my decision affect me and other people? Will it be helpful or harmful?"

Remember that it is important to avoid making any decision that could harm you or other people.

Guideline Three. Answer the question as soon as possible.

Once you know the answer to a question, tell you answer to the person who asked the question.

Do not make the person wait any longer than necessary.

Do not let anyone believe you are going to say yes when you are going to say no.

And do not let anyone believe you are going to say no when you are going to say yes.

Guideline Four. Be clear.

Some people might avoid saying the word "no" by:
- pretending that they were not asked the question,
- refusing to give an answer to the question,
- getting upset because they were asked the question, or
- giving all the reasons they want to say no without actually saying no.

Because these actions can be misunderstood, they should not be used to communicate the word "no."

If your answer to a question is no, you need to say it. Saying the word "no" is the only way people can be absolutely sure that you mean no.

Guideline Five. Be reasonable.

If you have good reasons for saying no, it is good to share them with the other person. This might help the person understand why you are saying no and help him or her accept your answer.

Sometimes you might not know the reasons for your decision, or might not want to share them with anyone. In either situation, you do not have to give your reasons.

Give your reasons only if you know exactly what they are, or it will be helpful to you or others to share them.

Guideline Six. Be kind.

It is important to be kind when you tell a person no.

You can be kind by speaking kindly. Avoid talking loudly and avoid saying mean things.

You can also be kind by adding some kind words to your "no" answer.

Here are three examples of kind words you can add.

Example #1: "No, thank you."

Example #2: "No, maybe some other time."

Example #3: "I'm sorry, but no."

IMPORTANT SAYINGS THAT RELATE TO SAYING NO

There are several important sayings that relate to saying no.

First saying: "Never say 'no' if you can possibly say 'yes.'"

This means that because you often make others happy when you say yes, you should say it whenever possible.

Second saying: "Let your 'yes' be 'yes' and your 'no' be 'no.'"

This means that you should do your best to stay with the decision you make. Try not to change your mind too often, since this can confuse and frustrate you as well as the people around you.

Third saying: "There is no law against changing your mind."

This means that it is OK for you to occasionally change your mind. If you discover new facts or have new feelings that prove you made a wrong decision, you should change your decision. However, if you need to change your decision it is important for you to think carefully so that you new decision will be correct.

Fourth saying: "You can please some of the people all of the time and all of the people some of the time, but you can't please all of the people all of the time.

This means that it is impossible to make everybody happy all of the time. Therefore, you should not feel bad when, on occasion, another person is disappointed by a decision you make.

IMPORTANT SAYINGS THAT RELATE TO SAYING NO

Fifth saying: "Turnabout is fair play."

This means that if you have a right to do something, other people have the right to do the same thing. If you have a right to say no, other people have a right to say no, too.

CONCLUSION

If you expect other people to respond in a positive way when you say no, you need to respond in a positive way when they say no.

CONCLUSION

If you say no appropriately, you will be doing the right thing for you and the people around you.

www.ingramcontent.com/pod-product-compliance
Lightning Source LLC
Chambersburg PA
CBHW081408070526
44583CB00020B/2723